FOREVER

#Livethemoments

To:

From:

Published by Homefront Girl® Ink
Newport, RI
WWW.HOMEFRONTGIRL.COM

©2016 Gaby Juergens. The book author retains sole copyright to this book and all accompanying artwork. No reproduction of any text or artwork is permitted without the written permision of the author.
All artwork and text by Gaby Juergens
All Rights Reserved
ISBN-13: 978-0692743966 (Homefront Girl Ink)
ISBN-10:0692743960

Juergens, Gaby

Recipe for A Military Wife
Printed in the United States of America

Dedicated

to "You"

may you always
shine and grow to
be true to
the girl in the
mirror... every moment
of every day.

XO Gaby

Recipe for a

Military Wife

By Gaby Juergens

HEART of the WARRIOR

— HOMEFRONT GIRL ®

1 Cup of adventurous spirit

Faith

Generous helpings of
Hope and Faith
she will need both during
every moment of
their story.

MILSPOUSE LIFE *not for* SISSIES

-HOMEFRONT GIRL®

1/2 Cup of grace under fire

Add two cups of Wisdom

MILITARY WIFE

TRY TO KEEP UP!

—HOMEFRONT GIRL ®

Add generous sprinkles of laughter!

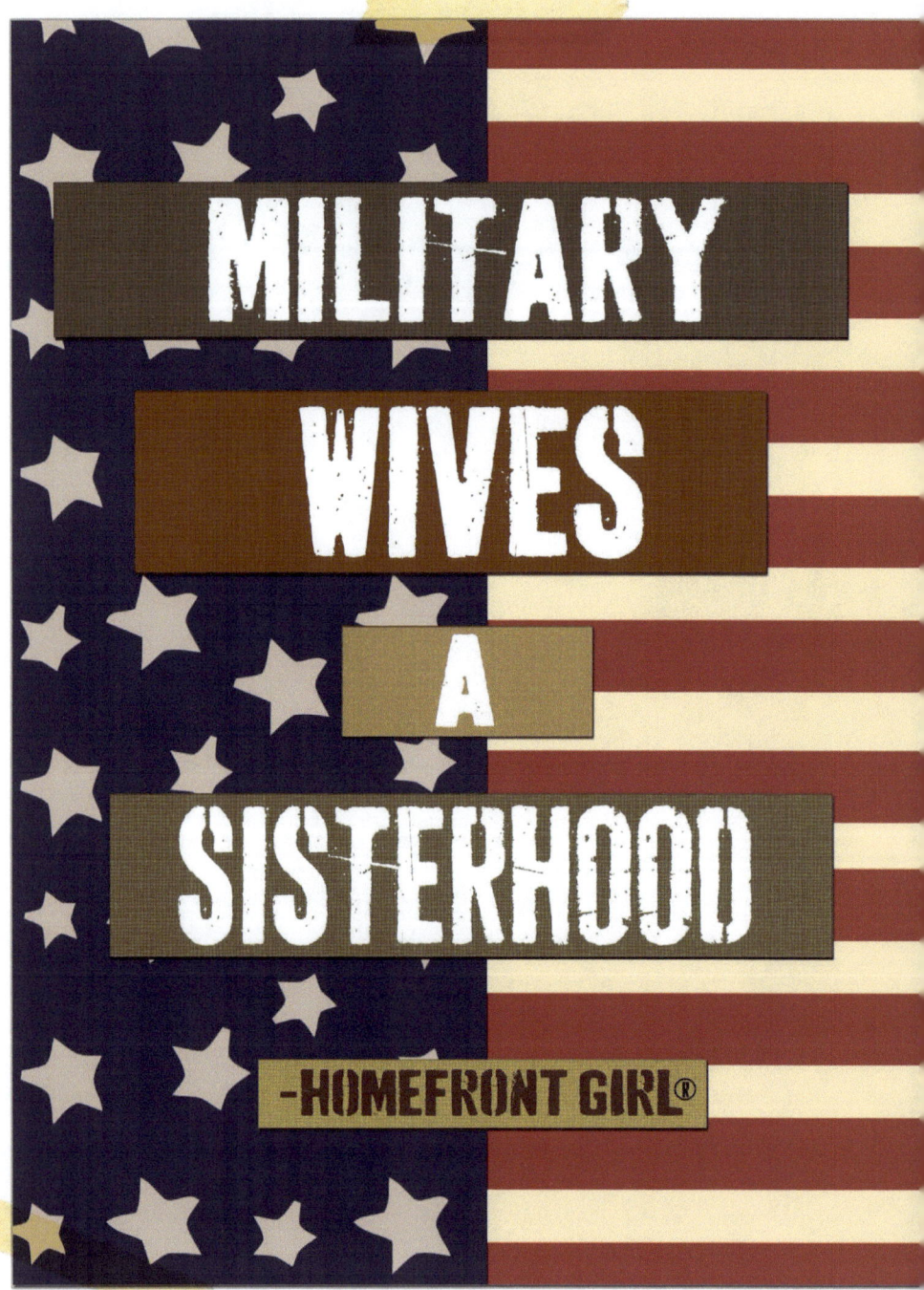

A few drops of gardening skills.
She will need to bloom in foreign soil...

Combine the ingredients

Add 2 Tablespoons of Generosity of spirit...

Fold in tears.

Both varieties... Happy and sad for she will experience both in full measure.

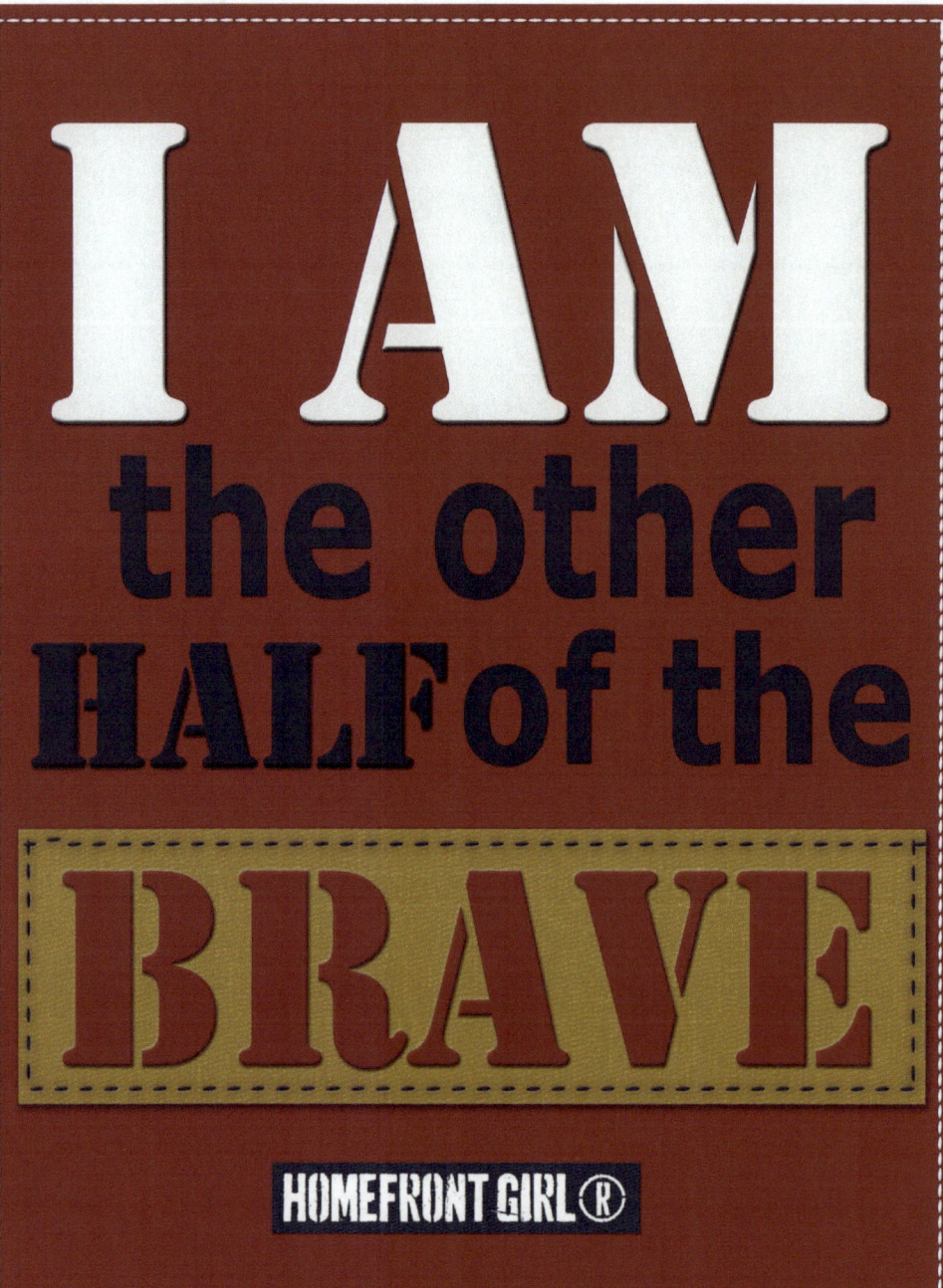

Yes. You are and always have been.

Stir gently.

So, not to upset the delicate balance of dedication to her loved ones call to duty...

ALWAYS wear **YOUR** SQUARED AWAY **CROWN**

—HOMEFRONT GIRL®

you wear it well.

Patience.
At its many demands,
and the sacrifices she will
have to make for Freedoms
sake.

BE STRONG

BE BRAVE

BE THERE.

HOMEFRONT GIRL ®

Because you are.
Never, doubt it. And you are not alone.

Challenges:

She will need to separate the good and the bad of her future challenges...adding a "dash" of perspective...

MILITARY WIFE

VOLUNTEER BRAVE

MENTOR

Her Dreams

CHOSE THIS LIFE

Grace under FIRE

No RANK, Just Strength

PROUDLY SERVING

HOUSEHOLD 6

HEART OF A WARRIOR

INDEPENDENT

HOMEFRONT GIRL®

Keep this close.

A Journey...

It's a journey she embarks on
as she contends
with what each "serving"
will mean to their story.

every time.

Expand:

Place in a small pan, but with enough room to expand her outlook.

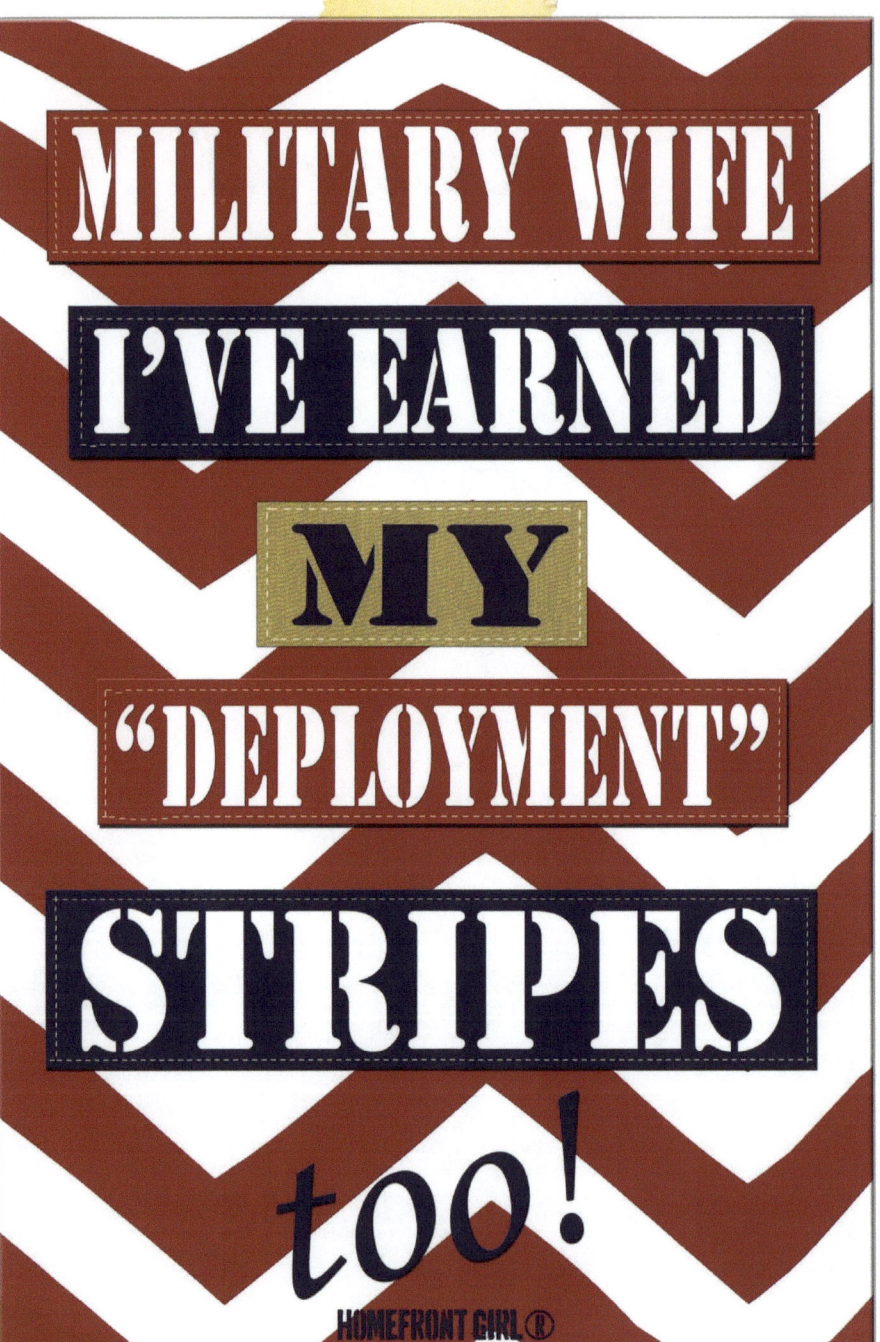

Every one.

Let her rise:

...and allow her to "rise" to the promise of following her own dreams.

Never lose sight of the hopes and dreams of that young girl...keep faith with her. You can do it.

Serve proudly.

She will grace any setting both at home and abroad with style and strength.

MILITARY WIVES
THAT TOUCH OF
Style
IN A WORLD OF
CAMO

HOMEFRONT GIRL ®

She's as unique and special as there are shades of camo in our world.

Yes, she does.

About the Author

Former military spouse, Gaby Juergens created her studio
after living the life for over 20+ years
with the objective every artist starts with and that is creating something
that connects the audience to the subject.
The Homefront Collection by Homefront Girl® is resonating
with those who share
and love their hero ...every day in countless ways.

A part of a series of "recipe" gift books.
"Recipe for a Military wife" was written
from the heart by Gaby.
Heartfelt and emotional, Gaby wanted
to capture the list of qualities that make each
military wife special, unique.
An empowering little gift book, it lends a voice to those
embarking on this journey to never lose sight
of what is your own story, as you follow
the fife and drum and a loved one who serves.
For a military wife serves as well...and beautifully.

Step forward and show the world how one of a kind
you truly are.

www.ingramcontent.com/pod-product-compliance
Lightning Source LLC
Chambersburg PA
CBHW041808040426
42449CB00001B/19